This book belongs to

Color With Me!

Grandma & Me
Christmas Treasures
Coloring Book

Sandy Mahony
Mary Lou Brown

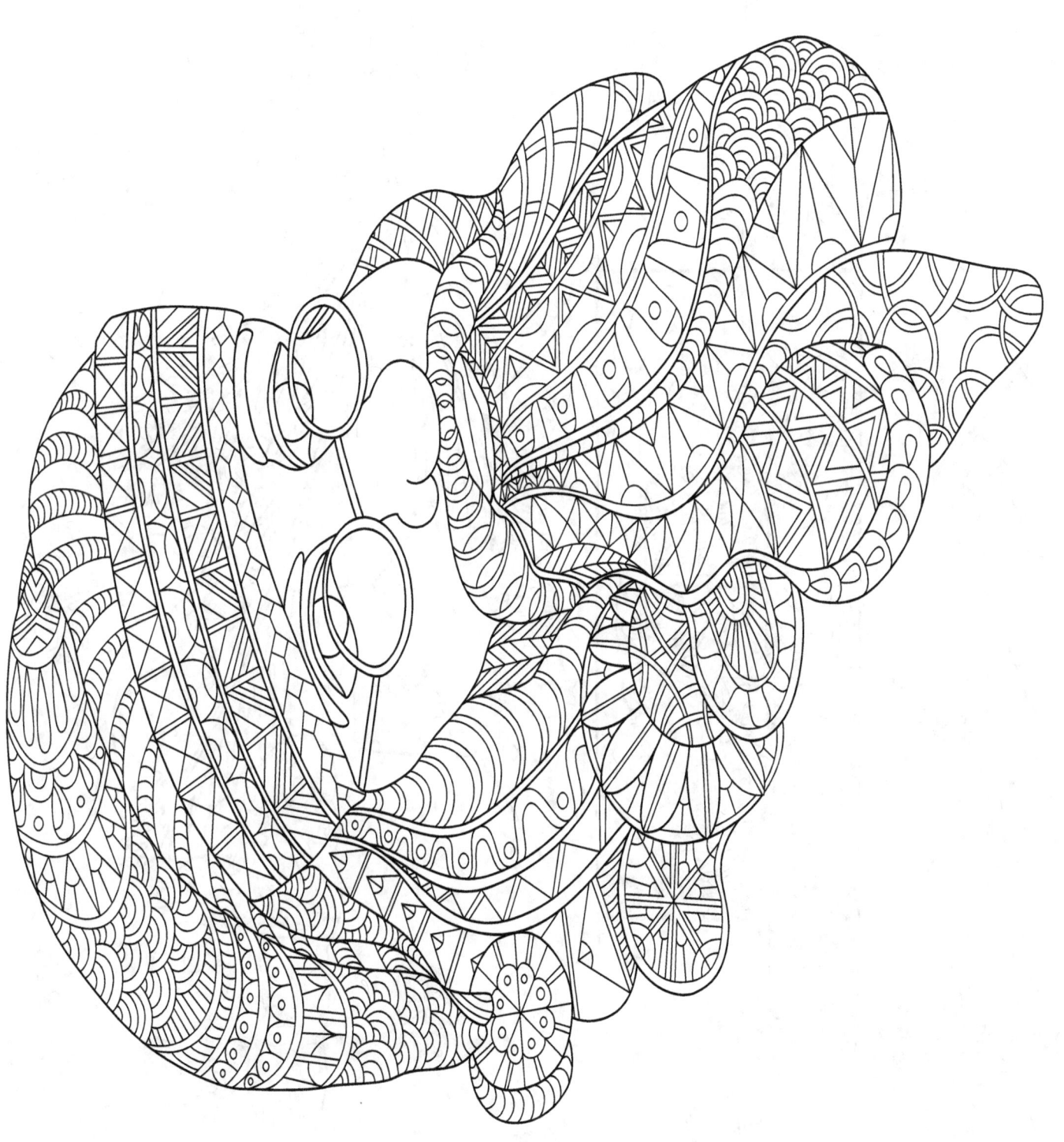

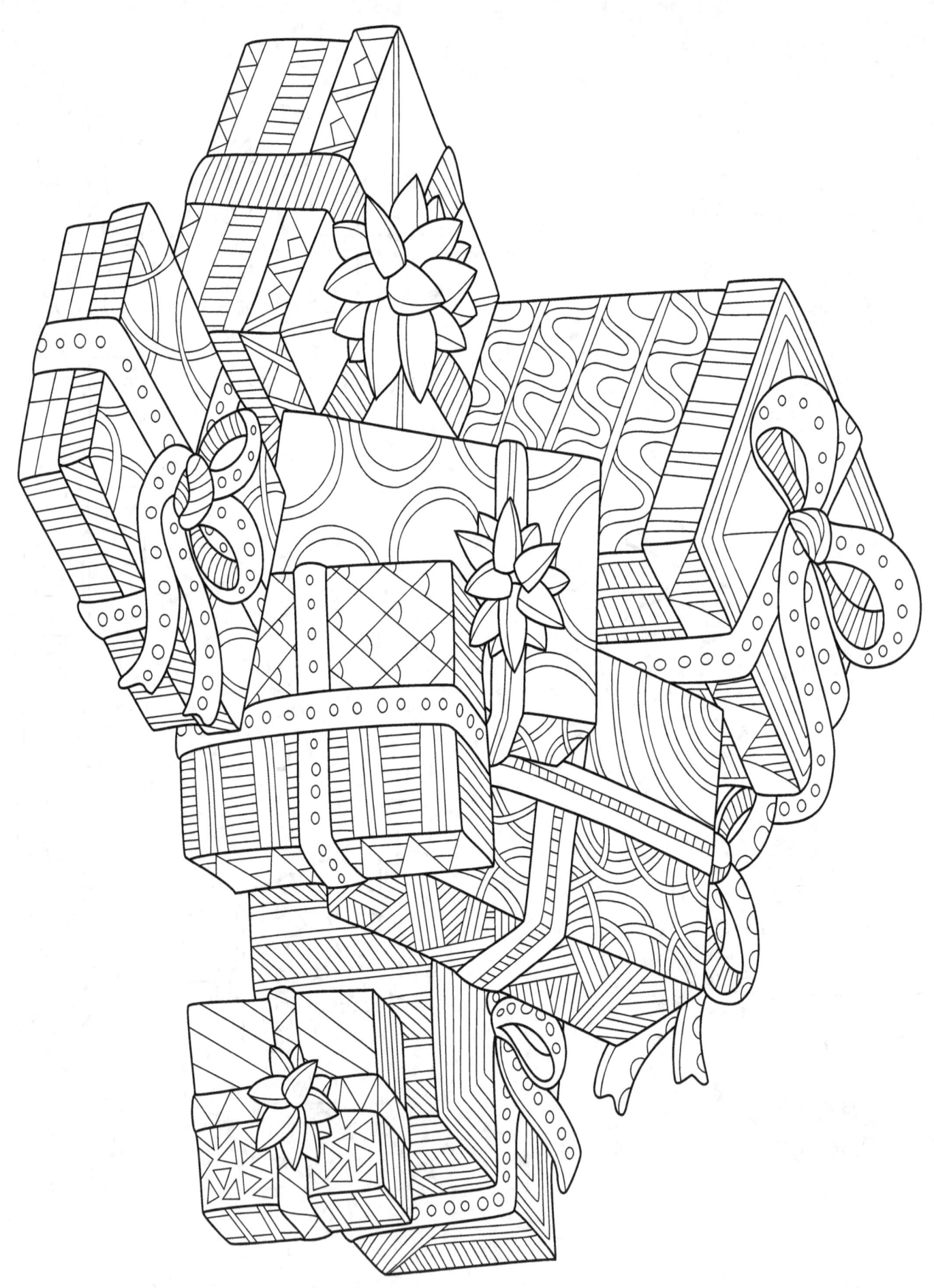

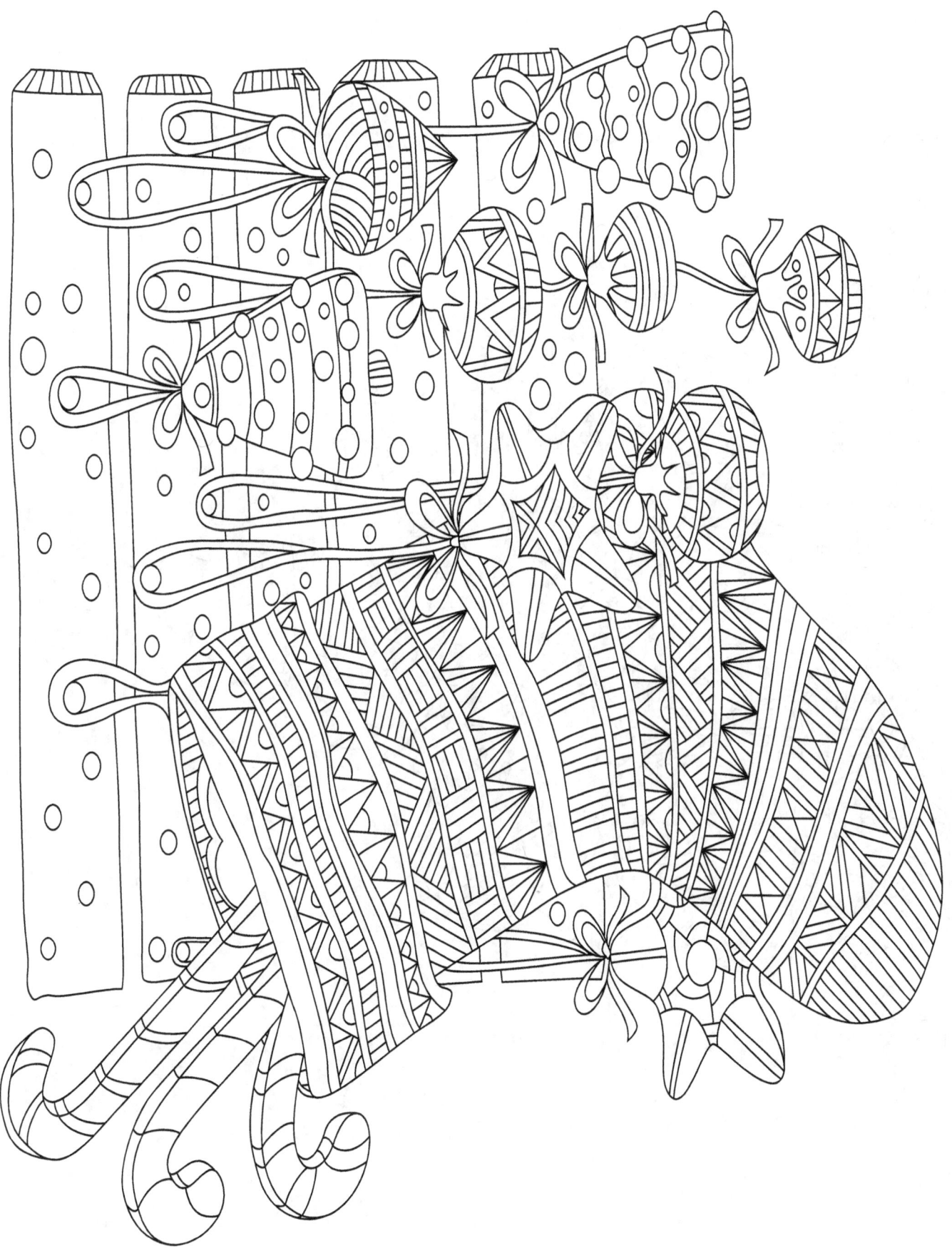

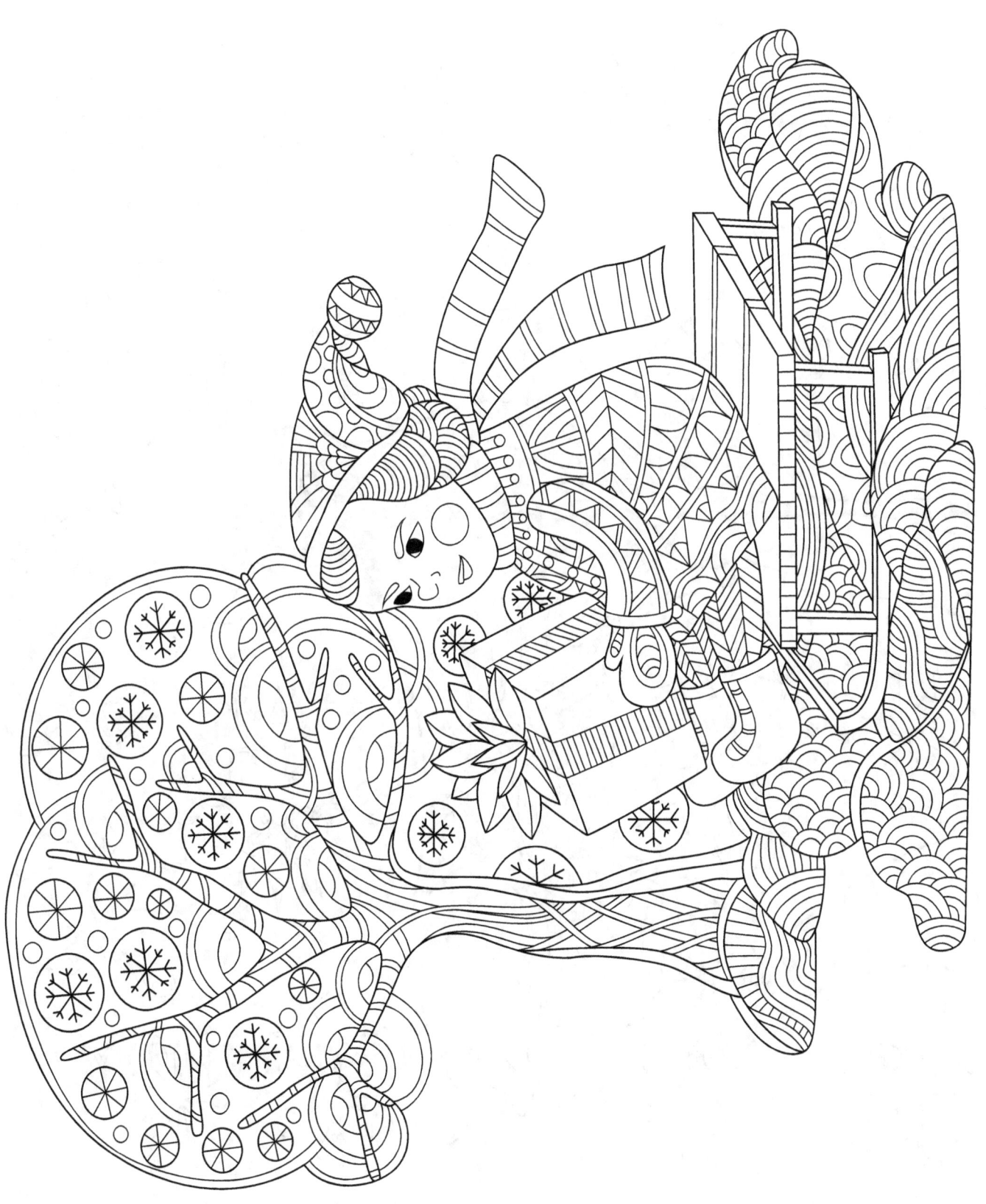

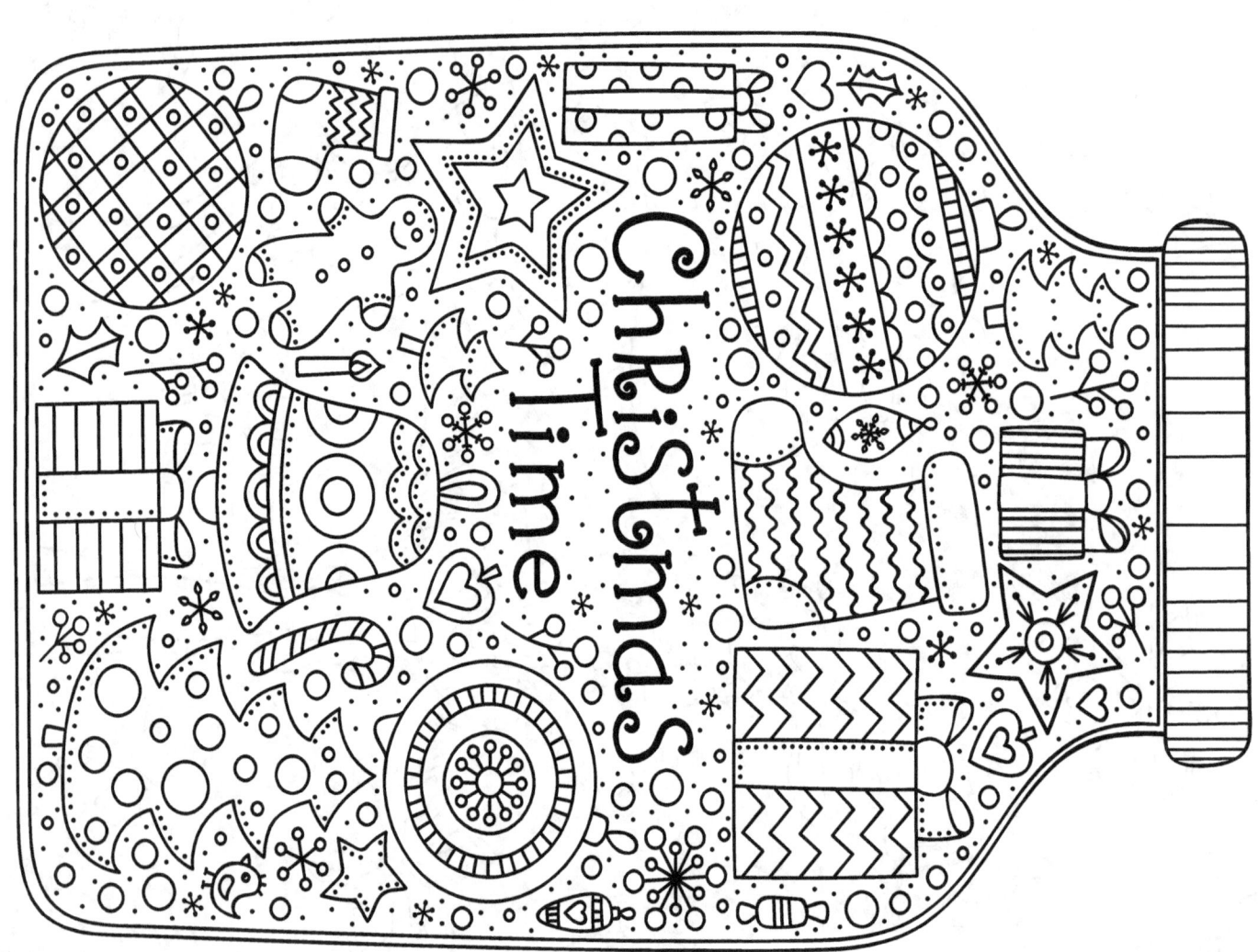

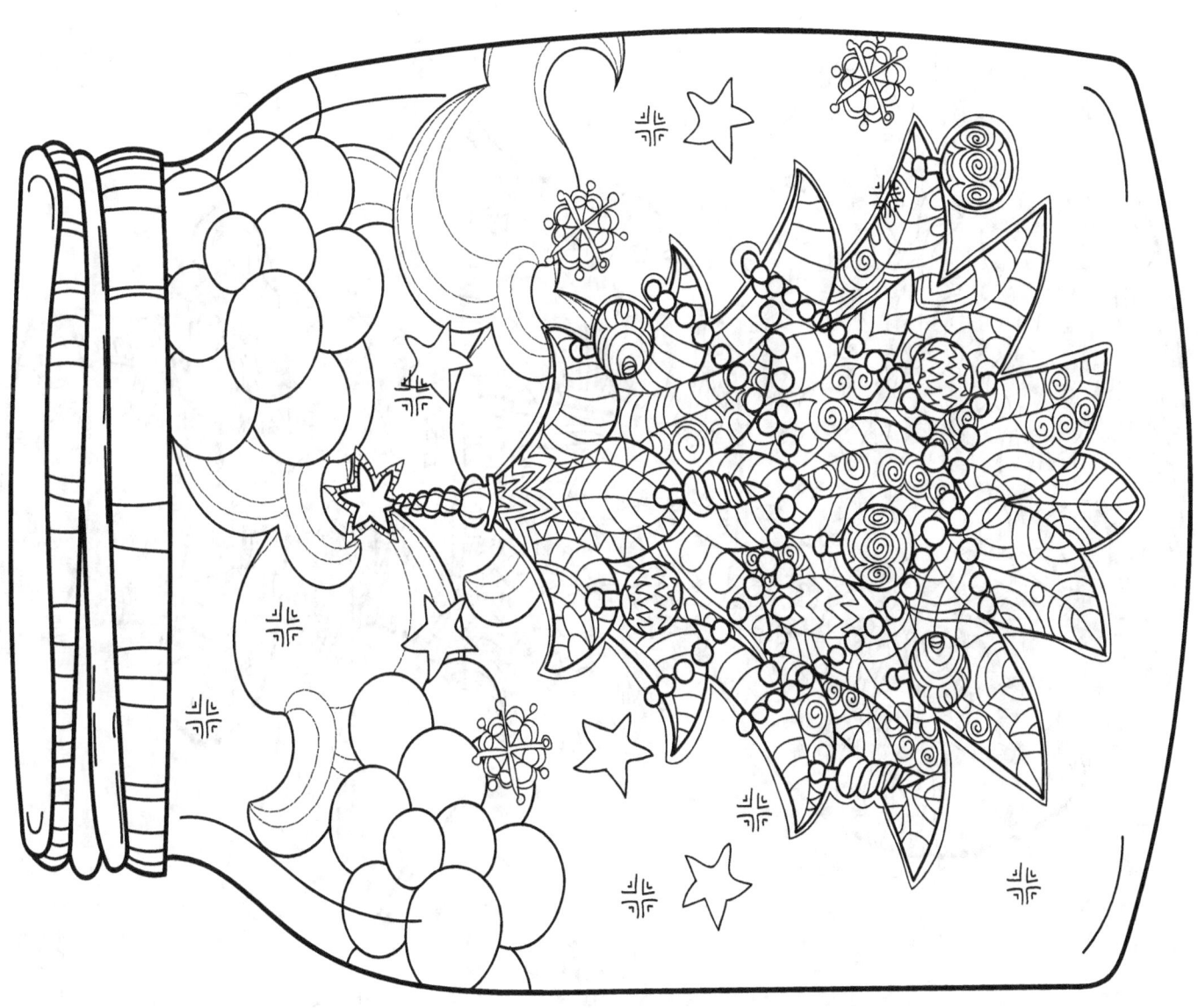

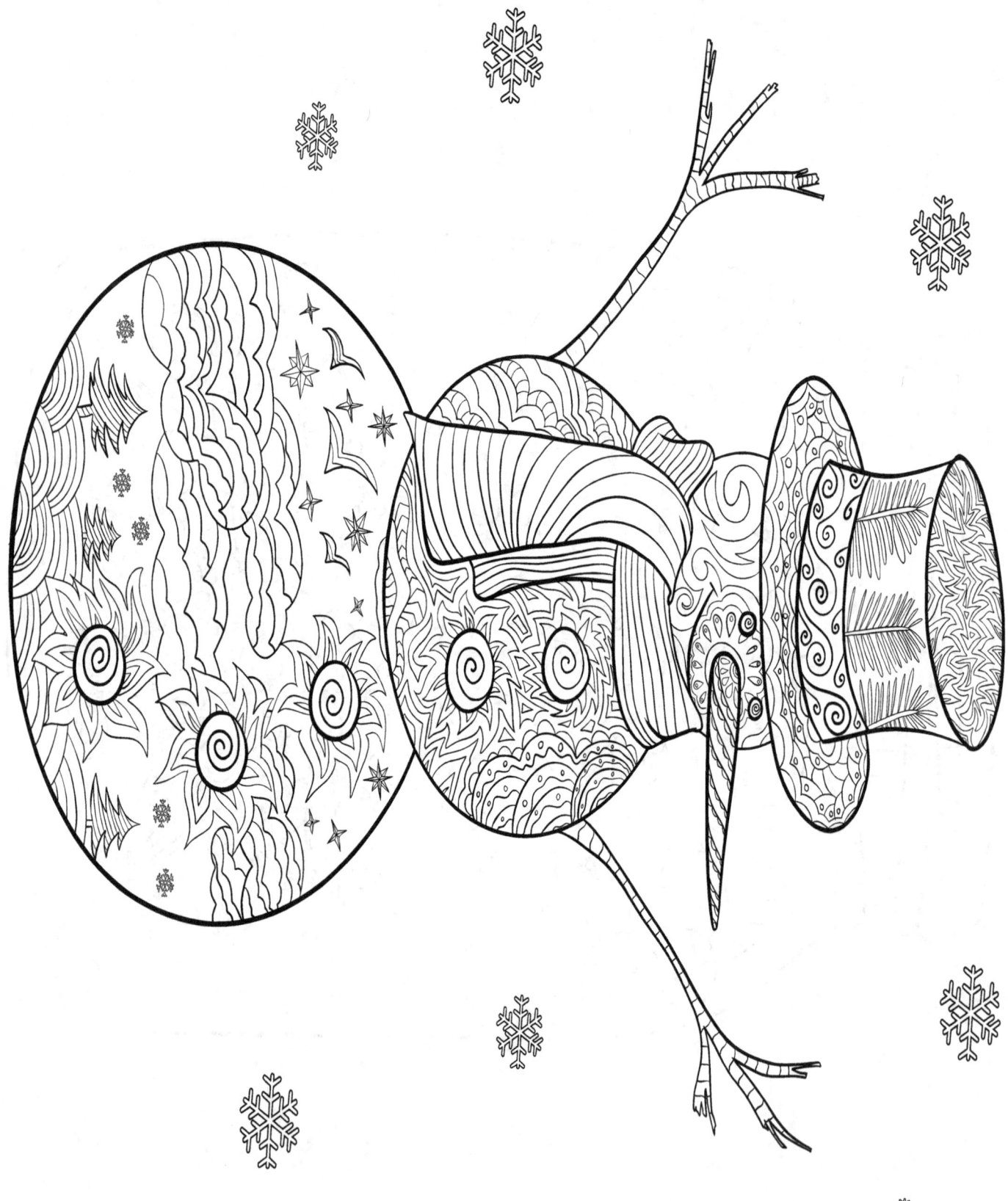

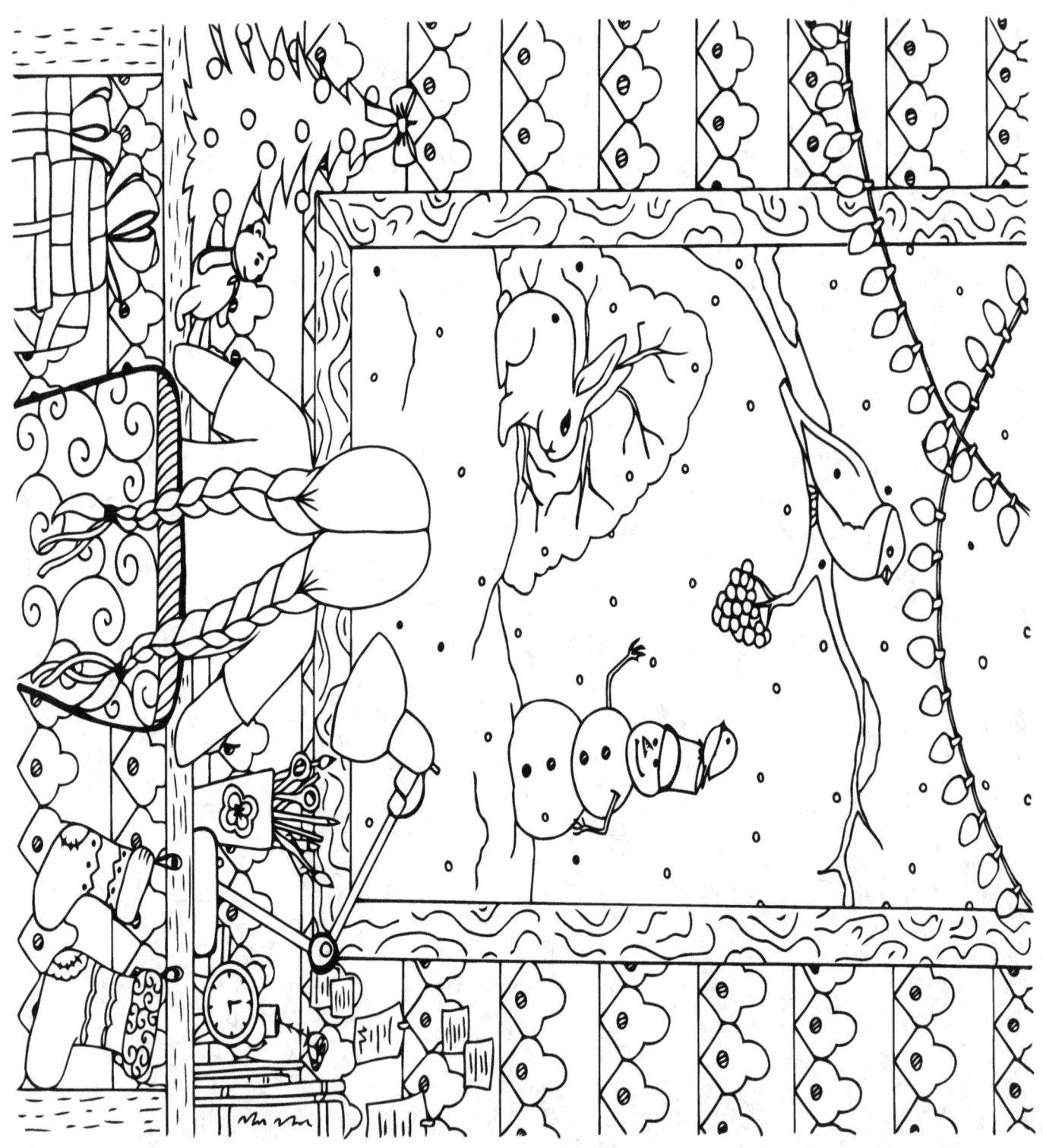

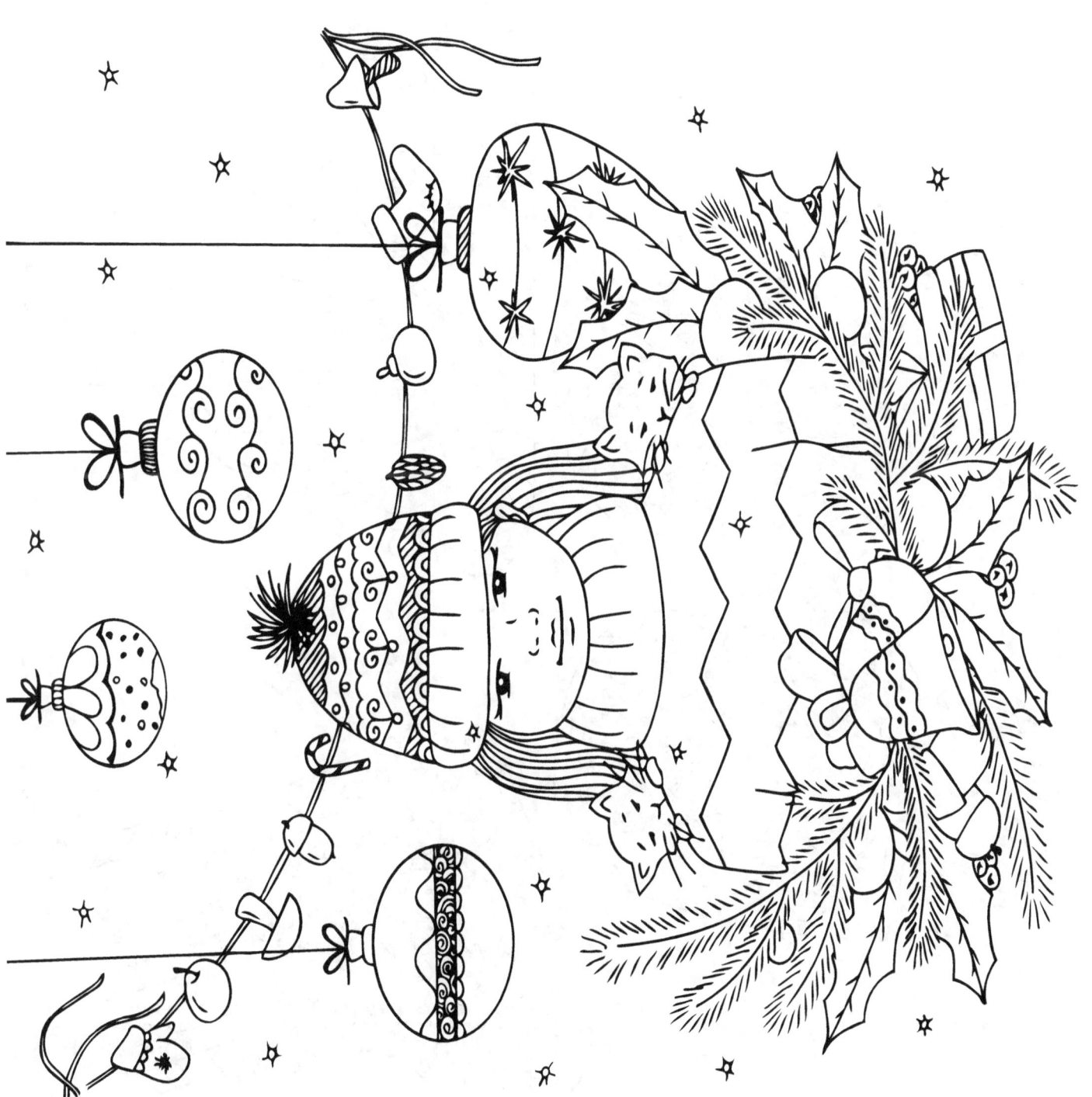

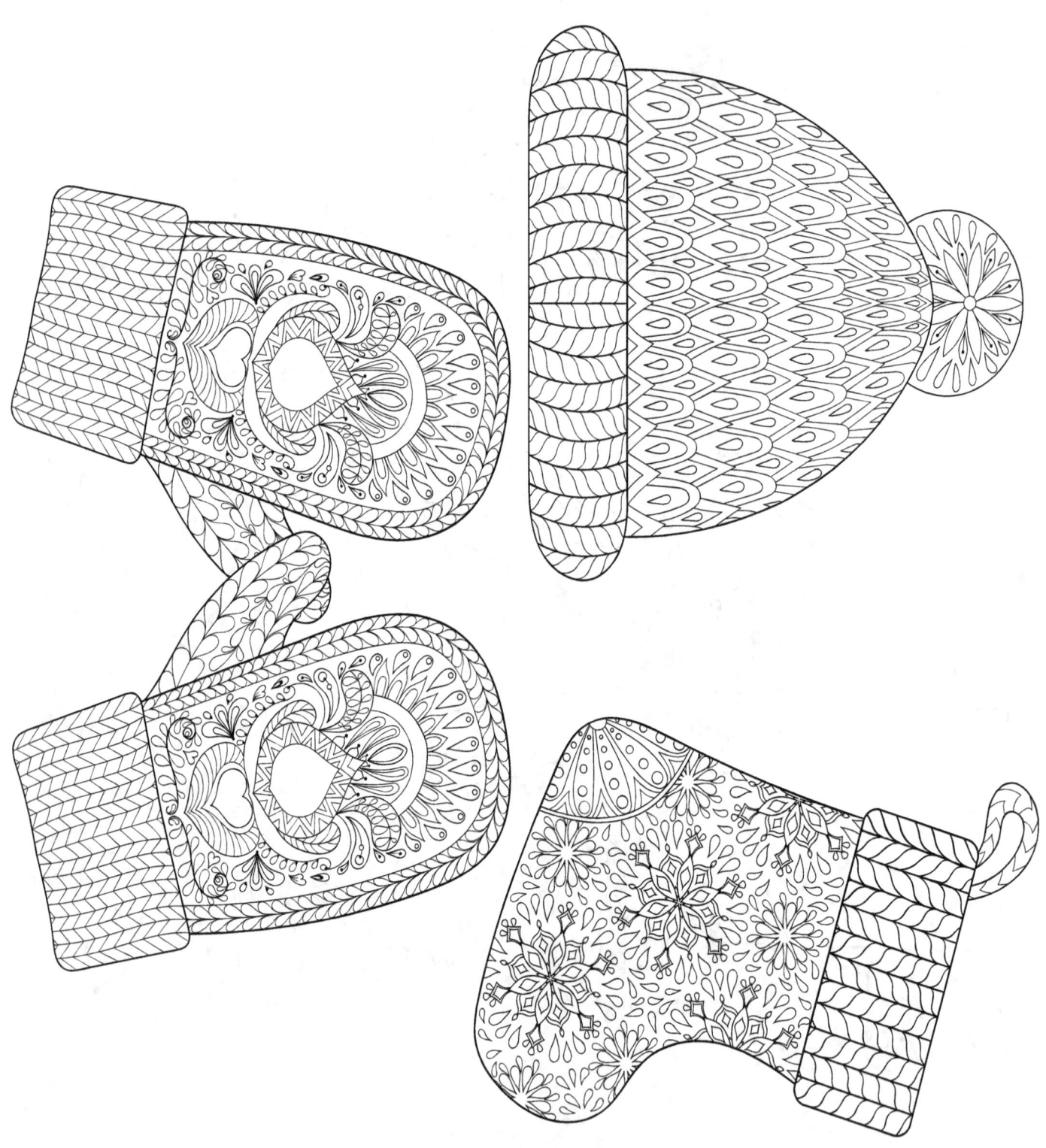

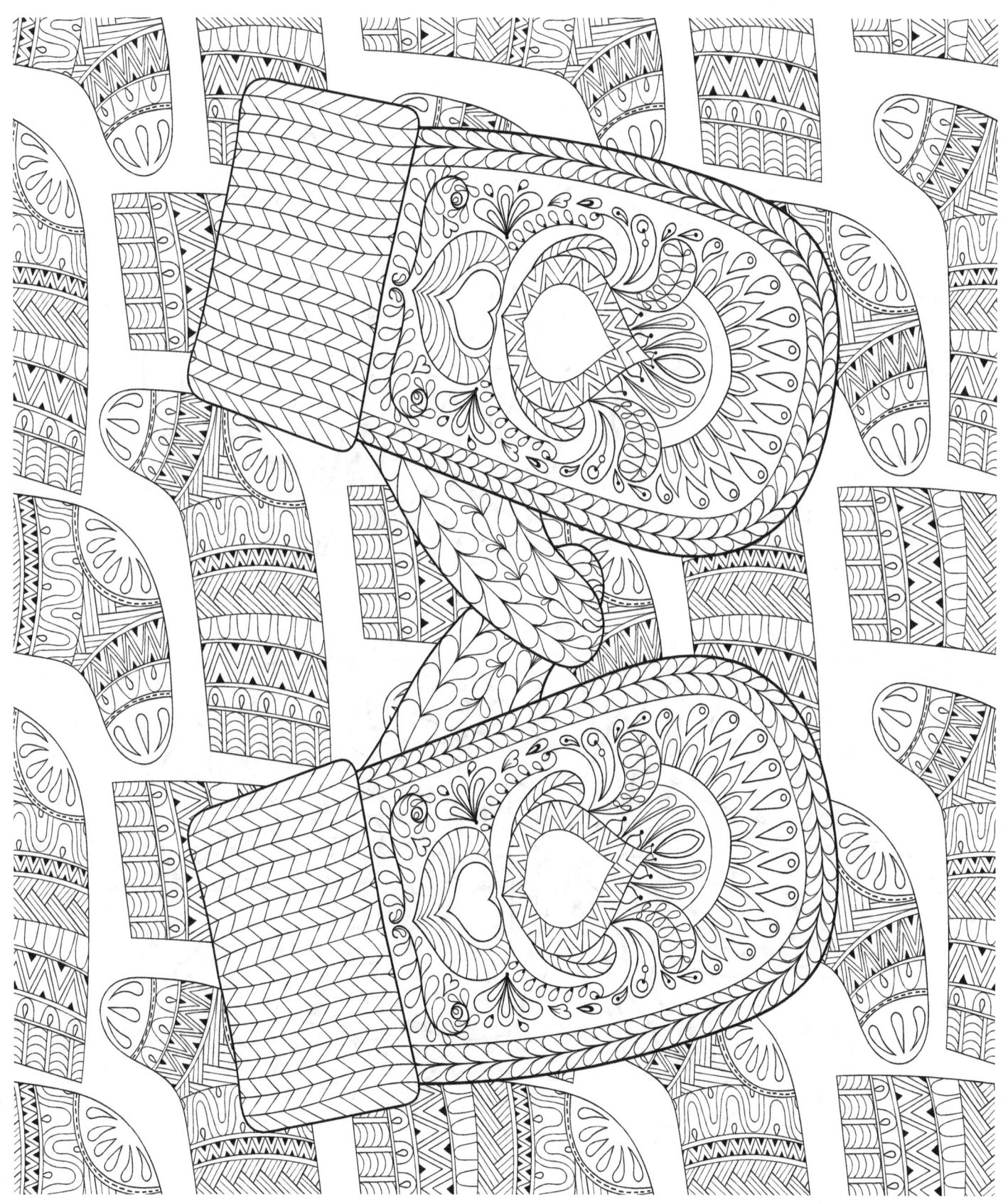

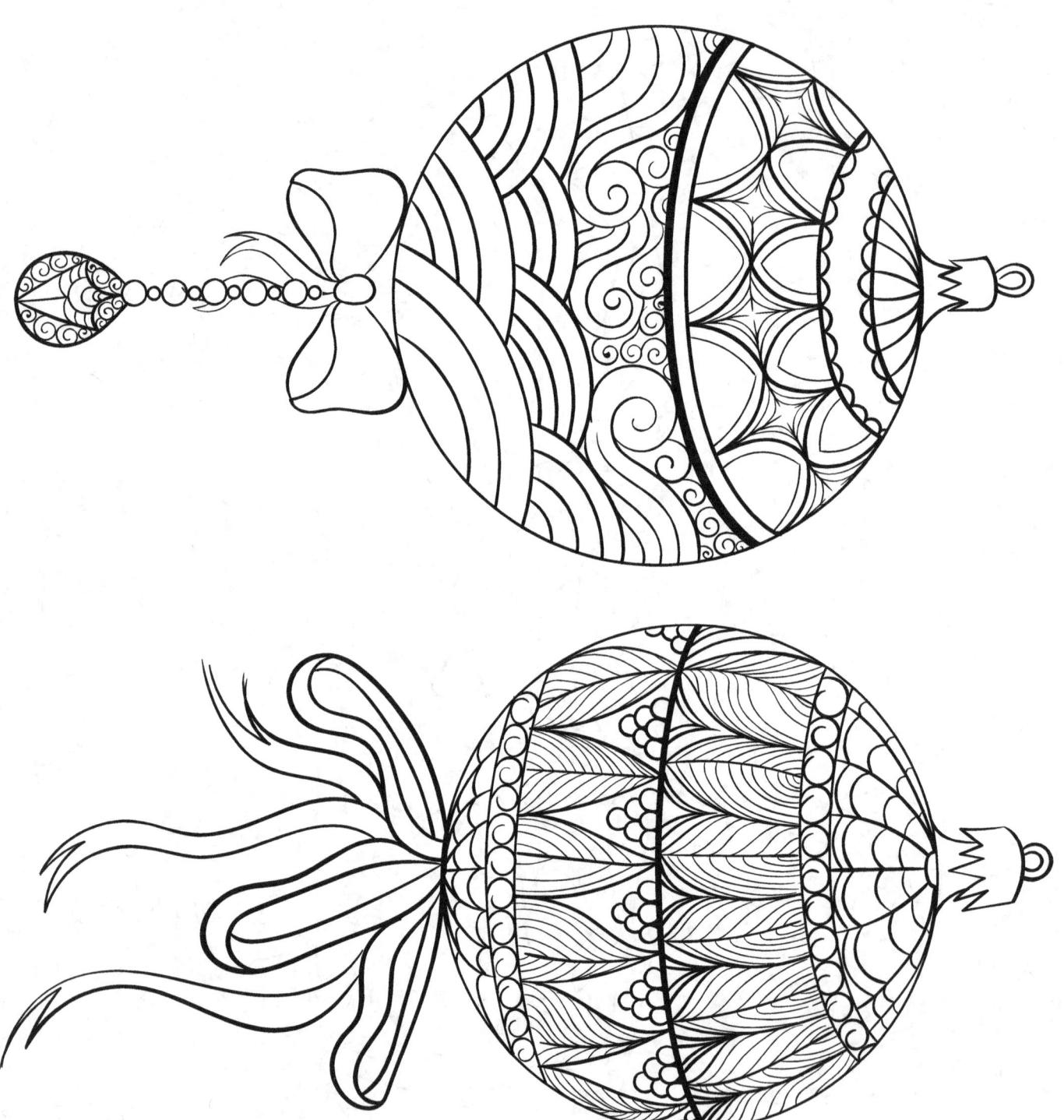

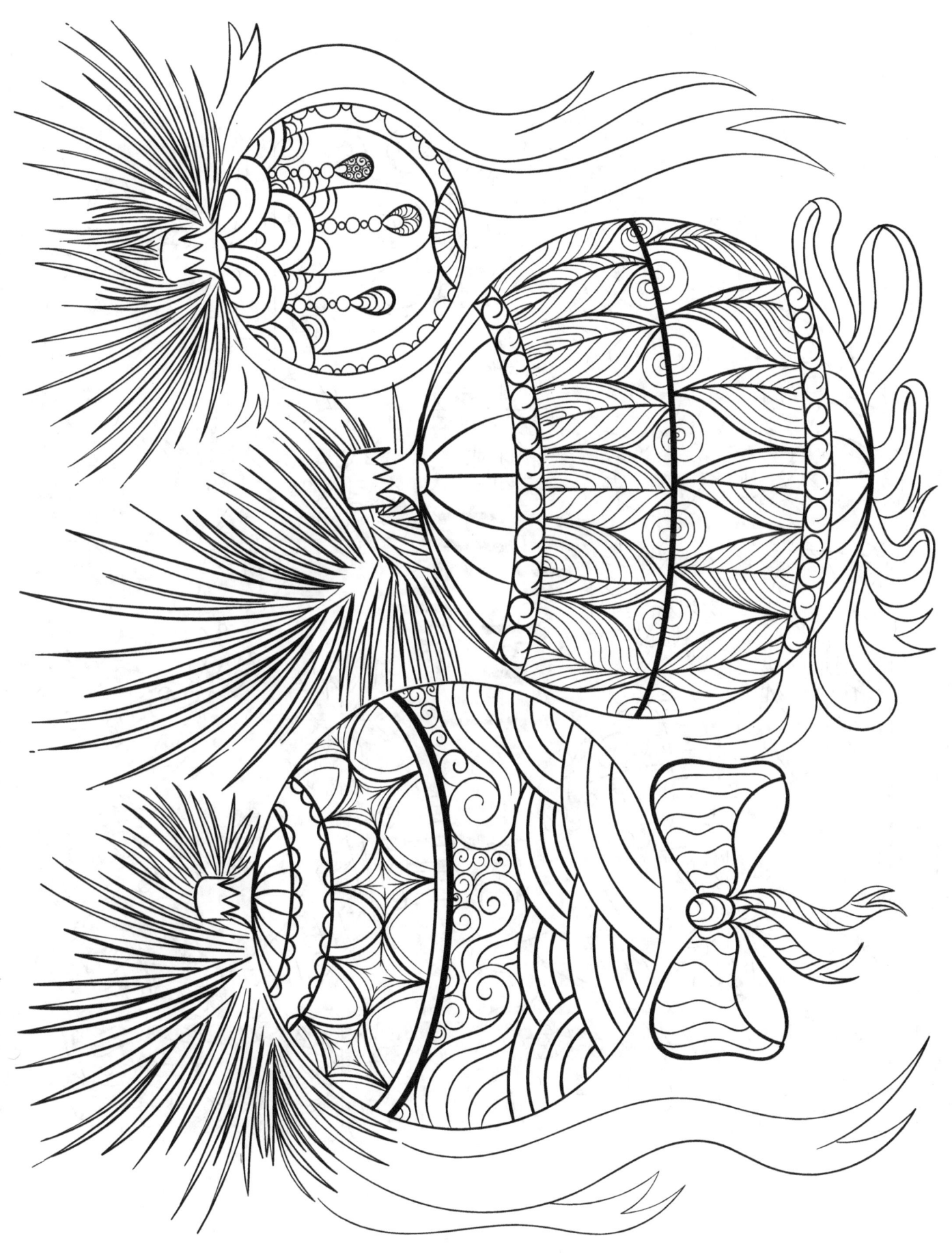

Winter!

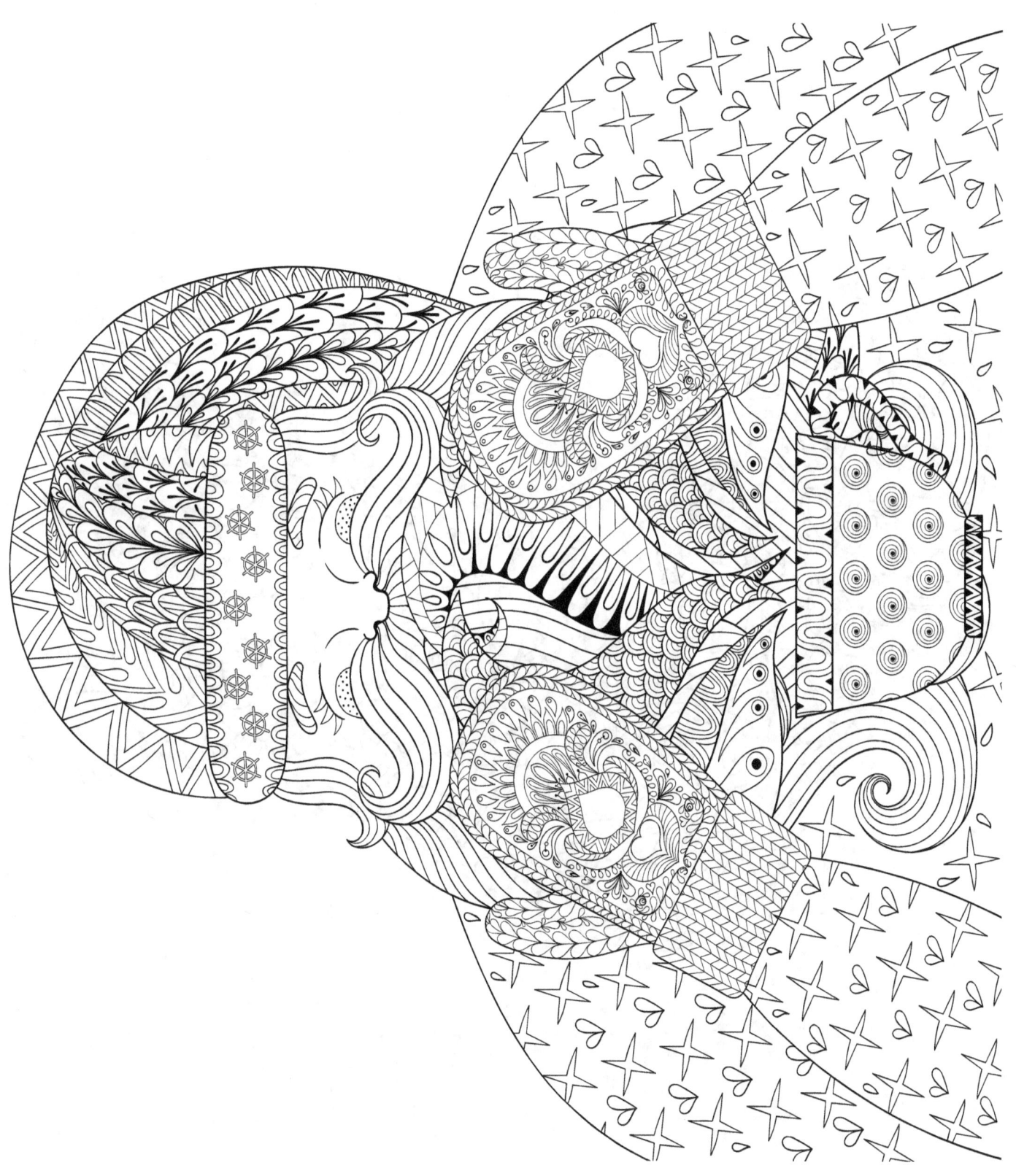

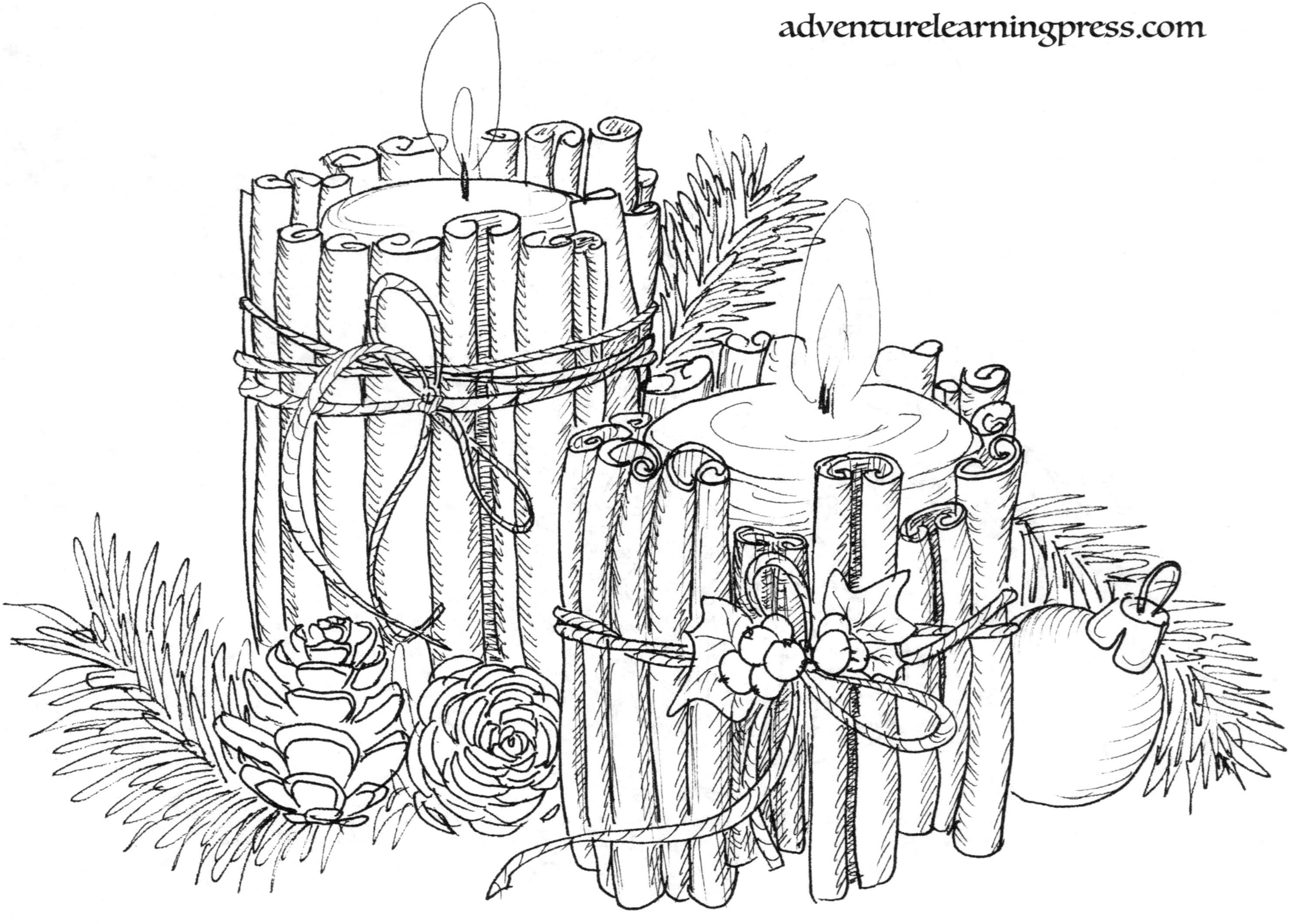

www.ingramcontent.com/pod-product-compliance
Lightning Source LLC
Chambersburg PA
CBHW081759280526

45789CB00008B/2919